Johann Gutenberg

VICTOR SCHOLDERER

Johann Gutenberg

THE INVENTOR OF PRINTING

Published by The Trustees of the British Museum London 1970

Printed in Great Britain at the University Press, Oxford
by Vivian Ridler, Printer to the University

List of Illustrations

IX   The first page of the 1457 *Psalter*, Fust and Schoeffer, Mainz, 14 August 1457.

X   The *Catholicon*, showing the colophon stating that the book was printed at Mainz in 1460, 'under the guidance of the Most High, who often reveals to the simple what he conceals from the wise', and 'without help of pen, stilus or quill but by the marvellous conformity of punches and types'.

XI   The *Missale speciale*, printed about 1473 in an earlier state, designed about 1454, of the smaller of the two types used in the 1457 Mainz *Psalter*.

XII   Part of leaf v. from the first edition of the block-book *Biblia pauperum*, printed *c.* 1465, probably in the Netherlands. Both text and illustrations were produced by rubbing the uppermost side of the paper over an incised wooden block moistened with water-based ink.

XIII   Leaf 8 recto, second column, of the first Dutch edition of *Speculum humanae salvationis*, printed *c.* 1471 at an anonymous press perhaps at Utrecht. The text was printed from movable type in a press; the illustrations, however, were added separately by means of blocks previously used in a block-book, and were printed not in a press but by the block-book process of laying the paper on an incised block and rubbing the uppermost side.

XIV   The earliest illustration of a printing-press, from *Danse Macabre* printed by Mathias Huss, Lyons, 18 February 1499.

XV   A section of the Helmasperger Instrument, a summary of the Fust *versus* Gutenberg lawsuit on 6 November 1455.

XVI   A hand-mould for casting type, in the Gutenberg-Museum at Mainz.

XVII   A hypothetical reconstruction of Gutenberg's press in the Gutenberg-Museum at Mainz.

XVIII   The same press, showing a two-column page after printing.

Johann Gutenberg

The multiplication of books by writing with the pen is a
slow process and peculiarly liable to inaccuracies, and the
desire for a more satisfactory substitute must have often
made itself felt through the ages among the literate. But it
was not until the fifteenth century of our era was nearly
half spent that we know of any practical steps being taken
towards devising some method of superseding the pen by
mechanical means of reproduction. It is noteworthy that
these efforts appear to have been made exclusively in
Europe north of the Alps, where the problem was evidently in the air for some time before its solution. Why
this should have been so cannot here be further discussed,
beyond suggesting that the greater ease of communication
between scholars in the climatic and cultural conditions
of Italy at this time may have caused the shortcomings of
pen-and-ink to be less urgently felt than in the North;
certainly the skill of Italian craftsmen was in no way
inferior to that of their Northern rivals.

It had long been customary, in the case of books bound
in leather, to impress upon the top cover the title of the
text within, or the name of its author, by means of brass
punches bearing the letters of the alphabet applied singly
as required, and the possibility of extending this method
to reproducing the text itself must surely have occurred
time and again to inquiring minds. These minds were on
the right track, had they fully realized it, but the practical
difficulties were of the most formidable, and appear to
have discouraged any attempt to overcome them for more

than a generation. There was, indeed, another possible method, that of cutting a whole page of lettering on a block of wood, in relief, inking it and taking an impression of it on a sheet of paper. This process was long considered as a forerunner of printing with movable type by bibliographers, who could point to a respectable number of so-called block books thus produced. The evidence, however, goes to show that even the earliest of these date from a time when printing with movable type was already well established, and it is clear that the wood-block technique offered advantages only in the case of popular texts of no very great length and no variations of wording for which there was a large and constant demand. Many of these texts were really no more than commentaries on the woodcut illustrations combined with them, as in the much-printed compendium of Bible stories known as the *Biblia Pauperum*.

The fact is that the problem of mechanical reproduction is conditioned by the nature of Western script, with its twenty-six alphabetic signs perpetually repeated in various combinations. The unit on which all mechanical processes affecting it must be based is the single letter, and no attempt resting on any other assumption could be expected to succeed. The Chinese printed books long before this was possible in Europe, and it has sometimes been assumed that the Far East exercised an influence on the West in this matter. This, however, is merely to divert attention from the true contribution of the Far East to Western book-production, namely the use of paper, which had been manufactured in China as early as the beginning of our era and had penetrated thence to Europe by the thirteenth century, largely displacing the much more expensive vellum. The Chinese script, with its host of ideograms, all of readily manageable size and each recurring but once in a while, is far easier to deal with mechanically than our alphabet, with its few, small constituents constantly repeating themselves. The ideogram is bulky enough to allow of carving in wood as well as casting in metal, and the alinement of ideograms in page-form can always be achieved with ordinary care. By contrast, the single letter of the West, in a type of book size, is a minute affair, apt to elude the fingers which handle it, and yet requiring to be available in quantity for the rendering of any con-tinuous text. How was this recalcitrant unit to be so far brought under control as to compete on equal terms with the productions of the copyist's pen? Much trial and error went to the solution of the problem, but it was solved and it is accepted that the man who achieved the desired result was Gutenberg.

Johann Gutenberg belonged to the family of Gens-fleisch, one of the patrician clans of Mainz, at the junction of the Rhine and the Main, the seat of an archbishop and a city of considerable importance in the fifteenth century; his full patronymic was Gensfleisch zur Laden, but he was ordinarily content to be known as Gutenberg after the house in which his family lived. Mainz was well reputed for the number and skill of its workers in precious metals, and many members of the clan, including Johann's father, Friele zum Gutenberg, were associated with the archie-piscopal mint. Gutenberg thus had an early familiarity with the goldsmith's craft, an initial advantage which has an important bearing on his invention. The exact date of his birth, like so many details of his biography, is un-known, but probably lies between 1394 and 1399. The intestine quarrels which continually distracted Mainz had in 1411 driven his father into temporary exile, and when, in 1428, the guilds succeeded in ousting the patricians from their civic privileges, the son also quitted the city. Settling at Strasburg, further up the Rhine, he preferred to remain there when an amnesty gave him the opportunity of returning home in 1430; the proceeds of several annu-ities, however, were still reaching him from Mainz. Two untoward events disturbed him in 1436, when he was sued for breach of promise of marriage and for slander. The lady appears to have been unsuccessful in forcing his hand and we have every reason to believe that he remained unmarried to the end of his days, but one of the witnesses in the case, a shoemaker named Claus Schott, had given evidence which Gutenberg resented, and which caused him to call Schott 'a poor creature, leading a life of lies and deceit'. This outburst, which cost him 15 Rhenish guilders in damages, is one of several indications that the aristocratic Gutenberg was inclined to carry things with a high hand: it was the more provocative in that Schott was a full citizen of Strasburg whereas he himself was never more than a resident alien. However, about this time Gutenberg was already trying out various technical pro-cesses, concerning which we are informed a little later by the earliest surviving pieces of documentary evidence re-lating to his activities in this field. They contain the testi-mony of the witnesses in a lawsuit brought against him in 1439 and the decision of the court promulgated on 12 December of that year, and may be summarized as follows:

Some years before, a citizen of Strasburg, one Andreas Dritzehn, had applied to Gutenberg to be instructed in 'several arts' and Gutenberg had taught him that of gem-cutting. Somewhat later, when there was talk of a great pilgrimage to Aix-la-Chapelle (Aachen), Gutenberg took into partnership a Strasburg official for the purpose of manufacturing certain articles to be sold to the pilgrims, and this partnership was soon enlarged to include both Dritzehn and two other persons. Gutenberg was the tech-nical instructor and the articles to be produced, evidently by some new process of his devising, were hand-mirrors, which would no doubt command a ready sale among the multitude. Work was immediately begun but was abrupt-ly broken off when it appeared that the partners had mistaken the date of the pilgrimage: this was due to take place not in 1439 but a whole twelvemonth later. To make up for this interruption in their time-table, the three subordinate associates suggested to Gutenberg that he should instruct them in certain other arts which he was known to understand but which he had hitherto concealed from them. Gutenberg agreed and a fresh contract was drawn up, according to which he was to teach them his new secret on terms which involved them in considerable expense. The contract was to run for five years, from 1438 to 1443, and it contained a clause providing that in case of the death of one of the parties, his heirs were not to take his place but were to receive 100 guilders in compensation, all apparatus and stock as well as the secret of the art itself to remain the property of the firm. This clause became operative almost immediately, as Andreas Dritzehn died at Christmas, 1438, in great distress of mind, since his affairs were in disastrous confusion and he felt sure that his surviving brothers would never agree with Gutenberg. His forebodings were justified, for Georg and Claus Dritzehn at once required Gutenberg to admit them to partnership in the room of the deceased, and when he refused, took the matter to court. It seems that they could make out a case for themselves because Andreas, who was an excellent craftsman but otherwise rather casual, had omitted to have the contract sealed in legal form. The document itself, however, was found among his papers and the court, admitting its validity, decided in favour of Gutenberg.

The carelessness of Andreas, however embarrassing to his partners, was a fortunate thing for posterity, since our knowledge of Gutenberg's experiments at Strasburg rests exclusively on the two documents reporting the lawsuit. It is true that much remains mysterious, for the partners were sworn to secrecy (there being no patent law to protect the medieval inventor) and therefore gave away as little as possible under examination; nor, for that matter, was the court concerned with the technicalities of the work. But one thing is quite clear, namely that expenses were very heavy. Loans of considerable sums were nego-tiated for Gutenberg, and Andreas Dritzehn himself seems to have invested more than 500 guilders in the con-cern. Moreover, hopes of success appear to have run high, as is evinced by the evidence of one Barbara of Saverne in the Dritzehn lawsuit. She had looked in on Andreas late one night and, finding him still at work, commented on the expense, which she supposed must exceed ten guilders. 'Don't be silly,' answered Andreas, 'why, if you had what it has cost me over and above 500 guilders, you would be settled for life; and I have mortgaged my pro-perty and inheritance.' 'But by Christ's Passion', said Bar-bara, 'if you fail, what will you do then?' 'We shan't fail,' said Andreas, 'before a year is out we shall have recovered our capital and then we shall be in bliss.' This heavy ex-penditure continued to be a feature of Gutenberg's activi-ties and it says much for his powers of persuasion that he found so many persons ready to help him financially. On the technical side we are only afforded glimpses of what he was doing, but we hear of the purchase of lead and other metals, of a press and of certain 'forms' (*Formen*, afterwards a usual word for 'types'), while—most signifi-cant of all—one Hans Dünne, a goldsmith, deposes that as early as 1436 he had received 100 guilders from Guten-berg 'only for that which pertains to printing'. When Dritzehn lay dying, Gutenberg, concerned that his secret should remain intact, sent for all the 'forms' then in being and caused them to be melted down in his presence, not without regret on his part, from which we may gather that he already had a prospect of success. He also sent a message to Claus Dritzehn instructing him to show the press to no one, and to dismantle an object with two screws so that 'the four pieces' should come apart; these were then to be laid on the press so that their purpose should not be apparent. Claus reported, whether truly or not, that he could not find them. Much has been conjec‑tured as to the precise nature of the 'four pieces'; possibly they constituted a forme, but this is no more than a guess. They may even more probably have been the components of a type‑casting mould. Only this is certain, that if Guten‑berg did succeed in producing any printed matter while he was at Strasburg no trace of it survives, and although this may possibly be due to the ravages of time, yet his results were not significant enough to justify the renewal of the five‑year contract, which lapsed in 1443.

It was no doubt about this time that Gutenberg decided to leave Strasburg. He was seemingly unable to find fresh capital there and even his private resources were very likely strained by the cost of his experiments. The last mention of him in the tax registers dates from 12 March 1444, when he paid excise duty to the amount of one guilder on the contents of his wine cellar, which was always well stocked (in 1439 it had contained some 420 gallons). As the next definite date of his career is 17 October 1448, when he was at Mainz, a crucial period of more than four years of his working life is entirely unaccounted for and conjecture is baffled; only one suggestion shall be men‑tioned here for what it is worth, and this is that he may have been in communication with one Procopius Wald‑foghel, a goldsmith from Prague, whom the archives of Avignon in Southern France record as having been resi‑dent there in 1444 and 1446 and as having taught the secret of 'writing artificially' to several persons, who ack‑nowledged that his art was entirely genuine and useful. His apparatus is described in terms which at once recall that of Gutenberg himself, and it seems evident that both men were working on similar lines. Waldfoghel, how‑ever, disappears as abruptly as he had come into view and no trace of any of his production survives. The Mainz record of October, 1448, shows Gutenberg yet again as a borrower, but his credit was now so much impaired that he had to find a surety for repayment, although the loan amounted to no more than 150 guilders. His powers of persuasion were, nevertheless, far from being exhausted, and it was apparently in or about the following year that he entered upon his famous association with another citizen of Mainz, a lawyer named Johann Fust, in the course of which the typographical method on which he had so long and persistently worked was at last shown to be a completely practical proposition. Our evidence for this is comprised in a single document preserved in the University Library of Göttingen—the record or 'instrument' formally supplied by the notary Dr. Ulrich Helmasperger to Fust of an oath taken by Fust on 6 November 1455 during a lawsuit brought by him against Gutenberg, and of the decision of the Mainz councillors before whom the case was tried. The record is not a full report of the proceedings but only a short synopsis, much of its 77 lines of text being taken up with formal phrases of the law, and the archaic German in which it is written is often very difficult to interpret precisely. However, we have nothing else to go upon and the information which it conveys may be summarized as follows:

In 1449 or 1450 Gutenberg received from Fust a loan of 800 guilders, carrying interest at 6 per cent, to be used in completing his work on his apparatus, this being pledged to Fust as security. Gutenberg might at any time redeem it on repayment of the capital. After some time, however, it appeared that the 800 guilders were insufficient and Gutenberg applied for a further loan. Fust declined but offered instead to advance Gutenberg another 800 guilders on condition of being taken into partnership with him for 'the work of the books'. Gutenberg accepted and seems to have steadily continued his labours until late in 1455, when Fust sued him for the repayment of both the loan and the investment, together with interest amounting in all to 2,026 guilders. The court decided that Gutenberg was under an obligation to repay the original loan of 800 guilders, plus interest. As Gutenberg was unable to do so, his equipment and stock passed into the hands of Fust, who thenceforward ran the press on his own account.

It is clear from the record that the work on the apparatus and the work of the books were closely connected and the question arises whether a body of print was already in being when Fust took Gutenberg to court. To this there is a ready answer: it must have been round about this time that there was put on the market the monumental folio Latin Bible often called the Mazarine Bible because the copy formerly owned by Cardinal Mazarin was the first to attract the attention of bibliographers, but more scienti﹨ fically described as the 42﹨line Bible from the number of lines contained in each column of its double﹨column pages. It is neither signed nor dated—Gutenberg never attached his name to any piece of printing—but the copy preserved at the Bibliothèque Nationale in Paris contains manuscript notes to the effect that Heinrich Cremer, vicar of St. Stephen's at Mainz, finished rubricating and bind﹨ ing it on 24 August, 1456. These processes would take some time in the case of so large a book (it is bound in two volumes of 324 and 318 leaves respectively), and if we allow for this we are brought sufficiently close to the date of Fust's action to be sure that when the case was heard the Bible was either already on sale or in the last stages of completion. There is no other book which meets all the requirements of the situation disclosed by the Helmasper﹨ ger record, and the long tradition which asserts the Bible to represent the decisive achievement of Gutenberg is beyond doubt correct. We are, however, immediately confronted by a problem of a different kind: if success was so near and the expectation of satisfactory profits from the sales of the Bible was about to be realized, why did Fust choose this moment to foreclose? Would not any reasonable person allow matters to take their course undisturbed, with the prospect of further sure returns in the future, rather than disrupt the partnership for the sake of an immediate gain? Fust has often been simply dismissed as the villain of the piece, scheming to pounce on his partner as soon as opportunity served, but there are other possibili‧ ties to be considered. One is that Gutenberg was, like so many inventors, an unbusinesslike person, intent chiefly on working at his discoveries, and that Fust, seriously concerned about his money, some of which he had had to borrow himself, and was paying interest on, sold him up because he could not be got to finish the job in hand; in this case Fust must have previously assured himself that he could rely on Gutenberg's foreman, Peter Schoeffer, to do what remained to be done as quickly as possible. Colour is lent to this view of the inventor by the fact that his earliest efforts dated twenty years back and that, when all allowances for the difficulties confronting a pioneer have been made, this rate of progress seems uncommonly slow—though it has to be remembered that the work may well have been subject to long interruptions. Recently, however, another explanation has been put forward, based on a fresh interpretation of 'the work of the apparatus' and 'the work of the books'.

According to this, the apparatus for which Gutenberg required his loan was the provision of several founts of type for printing some elaborate work in the shape of a church service book,* which would involve a variety of letter and proportionately heavy expenditure. The work of the books is not a general term but refers specifically to this project, 'books' being in fact equivalent to 'copies' (this, it may be noted, was subsequently a common form of printing contract). When Gutenberg had been for some years occupied on his task, it appeared that the time

---

* Whether the 1457 Psalter (see below) or, as has been suggested, a Missal for the use of Mainz.

Plate I The first page of the 42-line *Bible*, printed at Mainz about 1453–5, probably by Gutenberg, Fust, and Schoeffer. The illumination and rubrication were added by hand. British Museum C.9.d.3. *Reduced from 16 x 11 in.*

Si cui sane septuaginta interpretum
magis editio placet: habet eam a nobis
olim emendatam. Neq; enim noua sic cu=
dimus: ut vetera destruamus. Et tamen cum
diligentissime legerit·sciat magis nostra
scripta intelligi: que non in tertium vas
transfusa coacuerit: sed statim de prelo
purissime emendata teste: suum saporem ser=
uauerint. Incipiunt parabole salomonis

Parabole salomonis
filij dauid regis isrl:
ad sciendam sapienti=
am z disciplinam: ad
intelligenda verba
prudentie et suscipi=
enda eruditione doctrine: iustitiam
et iudicium z equitatem: ut detur paruulis
astutia: et adolescenti scientia et intel=
lectus. Audies sapies sapientior erit: z
intelliges gubernacula possidebit. Ani=
aduertet parabolam et interpretatio=
nem: verba sapientum z enigmata eorum.
Timor domini principium sapientie. Sapien=
tiam atq; doctrinam stulti despiciunt.

Plate II The beginning of Proverbs from the 42-line *Bible*, with illuminated initial
representing King Solomon. British Museum C.9.d.4. *Natural size.*

originally allowed for it would be greatly exceeded, and Fust, whose outgoings on the original loan and on current expenses were heavy, became alarmed. He was therefore prepared to give Gutenberg the second subsidy of 800 guilders which he now requested only if the conditions were changed: he himself was to enter the business as a partner and share in the profits. At the same time the pro/ gramme of work was modified. Gutenberg was now to put in hand immediately a more modest piece of printing, for which only the single fount of type as yet available would be required, and this was to be put through the press as quickly as possible, so as to yield an early profit. The book thus undertaken was the 42/line Bible, in which one type only is used throughout, and it was ready for sale about the middle of 1455; profits were expected to be very large. At this point Fust reflected that the realization of this part of the associates' programme would provide Gutenberg with enough money to pay off both principal and interest of the original loan and thus make himself master of the material on which it had been secured. With this in hand, his obvious course was to dissolve the part/ nership and continue printing on his own account, leav/ ing Fust with nothing to show for his speculations except his half/share in the profits accruing from the Bible. It was, in fact, a case of either Gutenberg or Fust, and Fust therefore foreclosed on Gutenberg while there was yet time to put him out and assure the continuation of so profitable a business as printing to himself. It may be added that even from the beginning there was likely to be no love lost between the two men, of whom one was an aristocrat and the other belonged to the new regime which had driven his partner's family into exile. Moreover, Fust may have had reason to suspect that Gutenberg was diverting to his own experiments some of the money advanced to him for the joint work.

Whatever theory we prefer, it is at any rate clear that

Gutenberg's hopes of a prosperous typographical career had vanished with the loss of the material on which he had worked for so many years. It is conceivable that the fount employed in the 42-line Bible remained in his hands, but this was ill adapted to any other purpose than productions of similar bulk and character, which were now completely beyond his resources. Two further types, on the other hand, which he must have brought near to completion, were taken into immediate use by Fust and Schoeffer for the achievement of the *Latin Psalter* dated 14 August, 1457, the first dated book ever printed in the West and one of the very finest. Gutenberg was at this time still in Mainz, as a notarial document of June of the same year proves, but we do not know what he was doing. He has further been credited with an edition of an immense Latin dictionary and encyclopaedia, the *Catholicon* of Joannes Balbus, which appeared at Mainz in 1460 and which proclaims itself as produced 'under the guidance of the Most High, at whose nod the tongues of infants become eloquent and who often reveals to the simple what he conceals from the wise'. These words, it has been argued, are such as might naturally have been employed by the inventor of printing himself; if so, Gutenberg succeeded in once more finding a moneyed patron, since the cost of printing an outsize folio of 373 leaves, in double columns, must have been very considerable. In fact we can point to such a patron in the person of one Dr. Conrad Homery, who on 26 February 1468, formally acknowledges return from the estate of the late Johann Gutenberg of what appears to be the complete equipment of a press, which was the doctor's property. Evidently Homery had at some time supplied Gutenberg with the means for resuming his labours, but what the latter may have produced, unless it be the *Catholicon*, we do not know; no piece of printing can definitely be connected with him after his breach with Fust. Indeed, very little is ascertainable about his later years. The loss of the lawsuit was by no means the last of his tribulations, for in the night of 28 October 1462, the Archbishop of Mainz, Count Adolf of Nassau, assaulted and sacked the city in pursuance of his feud with a rival claimant of the see, and Gutenberg may have been, for all we know, among the 800 citizens of Mainz summarily expelled from their homes next day. However, the Archbishop made amends when on 17 January 1465, he granted to Gutenberg the medieval equivalent of a civil-list pension by enrolling him among his suite, with an annual allowance of a gentleman's suit of clothing and of specified quantities of corn and wine, together with exemption from all dues and taxes. It is pleasant to think that the inventor was thus enabled to live out the brief remainder of his days in a respected position and reasonable comfort. Gutenberg died on 3 February 1468, and was buried in the church of the Mainz Franciscans. He was then about seventy years old.

Nothing is known of his personal appearance. The usual representations of him derive from an engraving made in 1584, which pictures him as an elderly man in a furred cap such as might have been worn by a Polish nobleman, with a forked beard and a rather vacant expression, the latter presumably due to the entire uselessness for typographical purposes of the die engraved with the first few letters of the alphabet which he holds in his left hand. This is purely a fancy portrait, if only because Gutenberg, as a patrician and a member of the archiepiscopal household, would have been clean shaven.

It has been noted that Gutenberg while experimenting at Strasburg protected himself by swearing his partners to secrecy. The same may have happened at Mainz, but a secret shared by more than two or three persons is not likely to remain one, and the printing of so large a work as the 42-line Bible, which gave occupation to no fewer than six presses simultaneously, was bound to afford to a considerable number of employees an insight into the new process, while differences between the heads of the estab-lishment made control more difficult. It is therefore not surprising that by the turn of the years 1454–5, as it appears, another press, equipped with a type similar to that of the Bible but rather larger and coarser, had begun to turn out a series of small works of popular appeal, in Latin and in the vernacular, including a number of editions of the elementary Latin grammar of Donatus. One of these pieces must be mentioned here. Although surviving only in fragments, it can be shown to have been, when perfect, a large broadside containing the German text of a plain man's guide to the casting of horoscopes, calculated from the position of the stars during the year 1448. It was first brought to light in 1901, and its dis-coverer, mistaking the nature of the text, called it an Astronomical Calendar and assumed it to have been printed as well as drawn up in 1448, which would have made it the first known product of Gutenberg's skill. But this assumption is irreconcilably at variance with its type, the state of which puts it unquestionably among the very latest examples of the group to which it belongs and brings it down to about 1458. As recent research has shown that the text would retain a rough and ready validity for a number of years after its original calculation, this date must be accepted and any connection of the entire group with Gutenberg in effect ruled out. The printer, whoever he may have been, went on in his turn to complete a Latin Bible, known as the 36-line Bible, some two years later at Bamberg; this also has been claimed for Gutenberg, but there is no proof of it.

Another controversy, until recently very much alive, can now likewise be considered as laid to rest. It concerns a folio volume of no great compass containing the service of the Mass in a shortened form and printed with a type identical, except for a few details, with one of the two employed by Fust and Schoeffer for the text of the famous *Psalter* of 1457. As the book was erroneously connected with the liturgical use of the diocese of Constance it was known as *Missale speciale Constantiense* or *Constance Missal*, although the correct and now generally accepted designation is, simply, *Missale speciale*. From the facts that its press-work is indifferent and that it lacks certain letter-forms normal in the *Psalter* two opposite conclusions have been drawn, one that it represents a try-out of the type before it was finally perfected for use in the *Psalter* and should therefore count as Gutenberg's first substantive venture, prior even to the 42-line Bible (which, of course, took much longer to print)—the other that, so far from being the first known product of Western typography, it is the work of some unknown craftsman of moderate resources and skill, who acquired a job lot of the *Psalter* type from Fust and Schoeffer after they had laid it aside and who printed the *Missal* with it as a speculation. Differences of opinion among experts as to the liturgical significance of the text further complicated the problem. Recent investi-gations by Dr. Allan Stevenson, however, have settled the matter by showing that the paper on which the Missal was printed was made about 1472–3.

Although Gutenberg's claim to be the inventor of printing in the West is now firmly established, it has not always passed unchallenged. A story long taken seriously told how about the year 1440 one Lourens Coster, of Haarlem in Holland, occupied himself during an after-dinner stroll in the local woods by cutting letters out of beech-bark, how on his return it occurred to him to set them side by side to form sentences, ink them and impress them on paper for the amusement of his grandchildren, and how ultimately, discarding wood for metal, he printed whole pages and gathered them into books. His secret was then betrayed by one of his workmen named John— whether Fust or Gutenberg the story left undecided—and carried by him to Mainz, where he reaped rich fruits from his theft, depriving poor Coster of the cash and credit which were his due. This account, which first appeared in print in 1588, gives itself away by the ease with which it glides from the use of wood to the use of metal for Coster's lettering. It is clearly unaware of the essence of the problem, which does not lie in the mere impression of inked letters upon paper—a very simple matter—but in the devising of a process which shall enable such impressions to be multiplied easily and quickly in the ordinary work-shop. A skilled wood-carver, in the course of a day's work, might—or he might not—produce a cluster of letters fitting well enough together to transfer to paper an impression not inferior to the work of an ordinary scribe. But meanwhile the scribe would outdistance him by several entire pages of text and the wooden characters would remain only a scientific toy of no practical value. The aim of Gutenberg, however, was to offer the reading public an article as well-looking as the work of the scribes and at the same time cheaper, and it was only by concen-trating his efforts on metal that he could meet these two conditions. When success came to him at last it was em-bodied in the type-casting instrument which stood at the centre of his process and which may be shortly described as follows. It is a rectangular mould of the exact size of the type required and opening on a hinge. At its base is inserted the matrix, a flat slip of metal into which the face of the type has been struck with a punch bearing the design cut in high relief. The mould is then closed and forms a tiny lidless box, which is then filled from the top with easily fusible metal (lead) in a molten state. In a matter of moments this has set hard so as to form a small metal stick bearing at one end, again in high relief, the design of the letter; the mould is opened and the type drops out ready for use. The mould being closed once more, the process can be immediately repeated, with the

certainty that every type so produced is of the same dimen⁄
sions as its fellows, to a hair's breadth. The whole opera⁄
tion is almost instantaneous and requires only a minimum
of skill in the manipulator. One other demand has to be
made on the instrument: since the letters of the Western
alphabet differ appreciably in width—'m', for example,
being three times as wide as 'i'—the mould must be
capable of adjustment so as to take any width of matrix
required. This was provided for by constructing it of two
L⁄shaped pieces which slid into one another along their
longer sides so as to vary the space enclosed between them;
this may have given Gutenberg particular trouble. A
minor addition was a casing of wood to preserve the
operator's hands from contact with the metal parts heated
by a succession of casts. It should be added that very great
care was required to ensure that punch and matrix were
worked exactly true, otherwise the resultant types would
print out unevenly or askew. But this would be guaranteed
by the high standard of die⁄sinking and other goldsmith's
work among German craftsmen in the fifteenth century.

Other matters, of course, must at various times have
claimed Gutenberg's attention, such as the quality of his
paper, the consistency of his printing ink (really a variety
of oil paint) and the structure of the press which was to
bring ink and paper into harmonious contact with his
type. But all this was subsidiary to the grand invention.
Not until he had perfected the type⁄casting instrument and
could make types by the thousand available at short notice
was he master of the situation and the manuscript of
commerce doomed. A copyist turning over the leaves of
the 42⁄line Bible must have been shocked to realize that
his occupation had suddenly slipped away from under
him, now that it was possible, in the words of a contem⁄
porary, to produce mechanically as much reading matter
in a day as one man's pen could manage in a year, with
the additional advantage, which no pen⁄work could

guarantee, that all copies, no matter how numerous, would show exactly the same text throughout.

Gutenberg's instrument continued in use, unchanged in its essentials, until the machine age was well under way. Its place is now taken by much more elaborate contrivances, but it was Gutenberg who set going the movement towards universal literacy which is one of the main conditions of the Western way of life. How far he himself realized the immense significance of his innovation is, of course, another matter.

Although Waldfoghel at Avignon is the only contemporary craftsman known to us whose work might be directly connected with that of Gutenberg, several other records must not be overlooked. The most important is contained in the so-called Cologne Chronicle, a history of Cologne published in 1499, which carries a personal interview by the anonymous author with Ulrich Zel, who had introduced the printing art into Cologne within ten years of its first successes at Mainz and was therefore a primary source of information. Master Ulrich is reported as saying that the right worthy art was first found out at Mainz on the Rhine in 1440 and continued to be investigated until 1450, a Golden Year, when printing was started upon a Latin Bible with a letter as bold as that now used for Mass books. He then goes on:

> Although this art was found out at Mainz in the manner in which it is now commonly used, yet its first prefiguration was found in Holland from the Donatuses printed there before this time. And from and out of these is taken the beginning of the said art and it was found in a much more masterly and subtle manner and the longer the more masterly it became. Item, one Omnibonus wrote in a preface to the book named Quintilianus and elsewhere that a Frenchman named Nicolas Jenson was the first to discover this masterly art, but that is a manifest lie, for there are some still

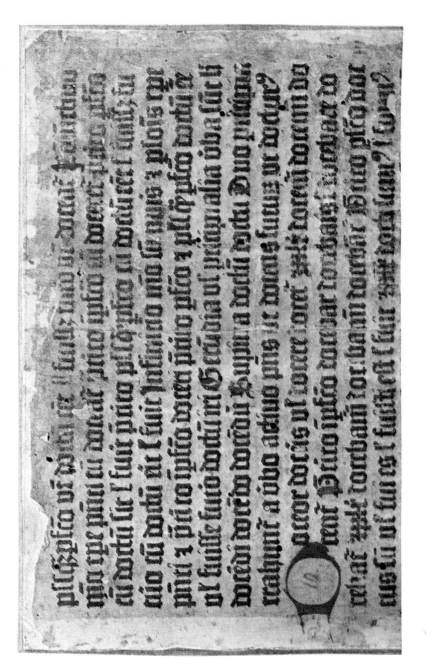

Plate III A fragment from an edition of Donatus's *Latin Grammar*, printed by an unidentified printer at Mainz, about 1455, in an earlier state of the 36-line *Bible* type. British Museum IB.66. *Natural size.*

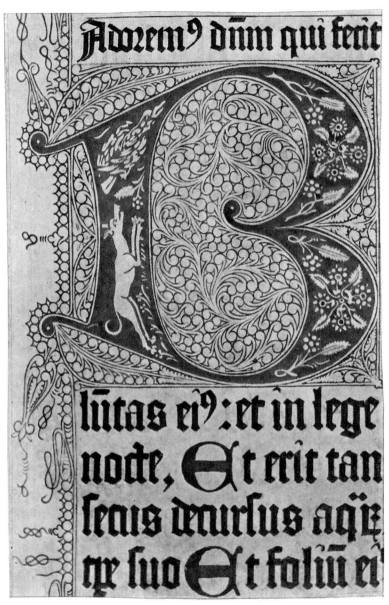

Plate IV The initial B from the first page of the *Latin Psalter* completed at Mainz by Fust and Schoeffer on 14 August 1457. The two-colour initials in this volume were produced from metal blocks, each constructed in two sectional parts which were inked separately, reassembled, and printed together with the text at one pull of the press. British Museum G.12216. *Natural size.*

living who can testify that books were printed at Venice before the said Nicolas Jenson came there and began to cut and prepare his letter. But the first inventor of printing was a citizen of Mainz and was a native of Strasburg and was named Junker Johan Gutenberg.

The interviewer was not an expert and one or two inaccuracies in the account may be due to him rather than to Zel himself; but unfortunately the latter seems to have been given no inducement to explain in more detail the nature of the Dutch prefiguration. He may well have thought that his questioner would make nothing of it if he did, but the loss is ours and we are left to conjecture to what process Zel was referring. His mention of 'Donatuses'—editions of the elementary Latin grammar of Aelius Donatus which was then universally used in schools— brings to mind the blockbooks, to which texts such as this, unvarying and in constant demand, were well suited, but it also links up with two entries in the diary of Abbot JeanleRobert, of Saint Aubert at Cambrai, of 1446 and 1451 respectively, telling us that in these years he bought at Bruges and at Valenciennes copies of another Latin grammar, the Doctrinale of Alexander de Villa Dei, which was 'getté en molle', but the second of which was so full of errors as to be worthless. The words 'getté en molle', although they might, it seems, be used of a blockbook, have been more naturally referred to some kind of metal stereotype plate, while they may seem less likely to be used to indicate movable type. More than this we cannot say. As for the untruthful Omnibonus (Leonicenus), his claim on behalf of Jenson as 'the admirable inventor of the bookish art, who first of all men showed how books were not to be written with the pen but printed like gems and resembling a seal' occurs in a book of 1471 and is obviously quite fantastic; at most it might be a confused report of some improvement in punchcutting or the like which Jenson could have introduced. It will have been noticed that Zel speaks of Gutenberg as 'the first inventor' and it may be that the craftsmen who were the first to intro- duce the new art into a particular city were also thought of as 'inventors', whom local patriotism and wishful thinking then exalted into first place; this would explain how the names of Pamfilo Castaldi at Feltre in Northern Italy and of others elsewhere came at various times to oust that of Gutenberg in histories of printing.

In view of the importance of the Helmasperger notarial instrument the summary of its main clauses given in the above narrative is supplemented below by those parts of the text which are of factual interest, in translation or paraphrase.

In the name of God, amen. On Thursday, the 6th November, 1455, between 11 o'clock and noon, there was present in the refectory of the Barefooted Friars at Mainz Jacob Fust, citizen of Mainz, on behalf of his brother, Johann Fust, also present, who set forth that in the suit of Johann Fust against Johann Gutenberg a term was set for this day, hour and place, for Johann Fust to take an oath in pursuance of the judgement delivered between the parties. And Jacob Fust sent to inquire whether Johann Gutenberg or anyone repre- senting him were ready to take cognizance of the matter. Thereupon there entered Heinrich Guntheri, sometime minister of St. Christoph's at Mainz, Heinrich Keffer and Bechtolff of Hanau,* servants of Johann Guten- berg, and declared they had been sent by their master to hear and see what was done. Thereupon Johann Fust, having again declared himself ready to carry out the verdict passed on his claim, caused this, with his plaint and answer, to be read out word for word as follows:

---

* Keffer subsequently worked as a printer at Nuremberg in the early 1470s; Bechtolff of Hanau is identifiable with Berthold Ruppel, who introduced printing into Basle in or about 1468.

And whereas Fust agreed, as stated in their written contract, to advance to Gutenberg 800 gold guilders for finishing the work (whether the cost were more or less) and Gutenberg was to pay him interest at 6 per cent, now therefore Fust borrowed the 800 guilders against interest and gave them to Gutenberg, but Gutenberg complained that they were not enough. So Fust, wish-ing to oblige him, advanced another 800 guilders over and above those in the contract, for which he had to pay 140 guilders interest. But Gutenberg never paid him the 6 per cent interest on the first 800 guilders as required by the contract, and Fust had to pay it himself to the amount of at least 250 guilders. And since Gutenberg never paid any interest on either principal, which in-terest he (Fust) had to raise among Christians and Jews, paying also 36 guilders compound interest, the grand total of principal and interest amounting to some 2,020 guilders, now therefore he calls upon Gutenberg to reimburse him this sum without deduction.

To which Johann Gutenberg made answer that Fust was to advance him 800 guilders so that with this money he should fashion and make his gear and that this gear should be pledged to Fust and that Fust should give him annually 300 guilders for expenses and also advance him workmen's wages, rent, parchment, paper, ink, etc. If they then failed further to agree, Gutenberg was to pay him back his 800 guilders and the gear was to be disencumbered. It being well understood that Guten-berg was to finish his work with his own money taken up on pledge, and he trusted that he was under no obligation to devote these 800 guilders to the work of the books. And although according to the written con-tract he was to pay 6 per cent interest, Fust had told him that he would not insist on this interest. And he, Gutenberg, did not immediately receive the 800 guilders according to the contract, and he was desirous to give Fust an account of the second 800 guilders. And he concedes to Fust no interest, simple or compound, and trusts that he is not obliged thereto by law, etc. Now therefore, all claims and counterclaims having been advanced at length, we pronounce judgment as follows.

When Johann Gutenberg has rendered his account of all income and expenditure which he has incurred on the work for their common profit, any money which he has received and taken in over and above this shall go to the account of the (first) 800 guilders. But should it appear that he (Fust) had given him more than 800 guilders not devoted to their common profit, he shall return this surplus also to Fust. And if Fust shall attest by oath or reputable witness that he raised the above-mentioned sum on interest and did not advance it from his own money, Gutenberg shall pay him this interest also according to the terms of the written contract.

This judgement having been read out in the presence of the above-named witnesses, Johann Fust made oath, with his fingers laid upon the Saints in my (the Notary's) hand, that everything contained in a writing which he then delivered to me was entirely true and accordant, so help him God and the Saints. And the said writing reads word for word as follows:

I, Johann Fust, have taken up 1,550 guilders, which were partly given to Johann Gutenberg and partly devoted to our common work, for which I have paid interest and compound interest annually and still owe a part. For every hundred guilders as aforesaid I reckon six guilders interest: for the money not devoted to our common work, given him according to the account, I demand the interest according to the terms of the judge-ment, and will maintain the truth of this according to the decision on the first article of my claim on the said Johann Gutenberg.

Of all the above-mentioned matters Johann Fust has required of me a record in one or more copies and all these matters took place on the said date in the presence of Peter Granss, Johann Kist, Johann Kumoff, Johann Yseneck, Jacob Fust, Peter Girnssheim* and Johannes Bonne, all men of good account. And I, Ulrich Helma-sperger, cleric of the diocese of Bamberg and notary public, have drawn up this instrument (written by another hand) and signed it and marked it with my sign manual.

This document, and especially the judgement of the court, is none too clear, but it seems that only the terms of the earlier of Fust's two loans were put into writing; the court took full cognizance of this contract, but there is nothing to show whether Gutenberg's offer to render an account of the second 800 guilders was accepted or not. From the amount of interest claimed by Fust it is inferred that this original advance was made in or about 1450, the second being agreed upon some two years later. On this reckoning the 42-line Bible was about three years in the printing, but preparations for the noble Psalter issued by Fust and Schoeffer in 1457 must have been going on at the same time and some part of Fust's 1,550 guilders was surely devoted to it. However, it appears to be impossible to arrive at any satisfactory estimate of how the money was spent; if it is at first sight startling to find that 800 guilders would purchase 100 fat oxen or several sizeable farms in the Mainz of the 1450's, we must remember that inven-tions are notorious for running away with the cash, while commercially that of Gutenberg was bound to be a fiasco as long as it was less than quite perfectly workable in all its parts.

---

* This is Peter Schoeffer, of Gernsheim, Fust's technical manager.

Selected Literature

BIBLIOGRAPHY

D. C. MCMURTRIE *The Invention of Printing*, Chicago, 1942. Other useful bibliographies will be found in the works by A. Ruppel cited below.

GUTENBERG DOCUMENTS

K. SCHORBACH 'Die urkundlichen Nachrichten über Gutenberg', in *Festschrift zum 500jährigen Geburtstag Gutenbergs*, Leipzig, 1900. The text in the original German, with notes.

O. W. FUHRMANN *Gutenberg and the Strasbourg Documents of 1439*, New York, 1940. The text in the original German, and in modern German, French and English translation, with important discussions of its significance.

D. C. MCMURTRIE *The Gutenberg Documents*, New York, 1941. All known documents in English translation, with reliable notes.

GENERAL WORKS

A. RUPPEL *Johannes Gutenberg*, Berlin, 1947. A detailed and well-illustrated study of all aspects of Gutenberg's life and work.

A. RUPPEL *Die Technik Gutenbergs und ihre Vorstufe*, Düsseldorf, 1961. Covers the whole field of Gutenberg studies, but with special attention to the technical aspects of his discovery. With numerous and important illustrations.

O. W. FUHRMANN 'The Invention of Printing', in *The Dolphin*, no. 3, New York, 1938.

V. SCHOLDERER 'The Invention of Printing', in *The Library*, ser. 4, vol. 21, London, 1941.

SPECIAL STUDIES

C. WEHMER *Mainzer Probedrucke in der Type des sogenannten Astronomischen Kalenders für 1448*, Munich, 1948. A work of fundamental significance, dating the 'Astronomical Calendar', with other works in various states of 36-line Bible type, to the period *c.* 1454–8. See also the the review of Wehmer's work by V. Scholderer in *The Library*, ser. 5, vol. 5, London, 1951.

SIR I. MASSON *The Mainz Psalters and Canon Missae, 1457–1459*, Bibliographical Society, London, 1954.

A. H. STEVENSON *The Paper in the Missale speciale*, Bibliographical Society, London, 1967.

Et ingreſſus āgelus ad eā dixit. Aue
gratia plena:dñs tecū:benedicta tu in
mulieribʒ.Que cū audiſſet·turbata eſt
in ſermone eius : et cogitabat qualis
eſſet iſta ſalutatio . Et ait angelus ei.
Ne timeas maria: inueniſti enī grati-
am apud deū. Ecce concipies in vtero
et paries filiū:ꞇ vocabis nomen eius
iheſum.Hic erit magnus:ꞇ fili⁹ altiſſimi vocabitur. Et dabit illi dñs de⁹ ſedem dauid patris eius : et regnabit ī
domo iacob in eternū : et regni ei⁹ nō
erit finis. Dixit aūt maria ad angelū.
Quomō fiet iſtud : quoniā virū non
cognoſco? Et reſpōdens angelus dixit ei. Spiritus ſanctus ſupueniet in
te:ꞇ virtus altiſſimi obumbrabit tibi.
Ideoqʒ et qđ naſcetꝰ ex te ſanctū : voca-
bit fili⁹ dei. Et ecce elizabeth cognata tu-
a:ꞇ ipſa cōcepit filiū ī ſenectute ſua . Et
hic mēſis eſt ſextꝰ illi q̄ vocaꝷ ſterilis?
Quia nō erit impoſſibile apud deum
omne verbū. Dixit autē maria . Ecce
ancilla dñi:fiat michi ſecundū verbū

Plate V The Annunciation (Luke i, 28-38) from the 42-line *Bible*.
British Museum C.9.d.4. *Natural size*.

maria · Et ingreſſus angelus
ad eã dixit·Aue gracia plena:
dñs tecũ:benedicta tu in mulie
rib; · Que cum audiſſet·turba
ta eſt in ſermone eius:⁊ cogita
bat qualis eſſet iſta ſalutacio·
Et ait angelus ei · Ne timeas
maria: ïueniſti eī graciã apud
deũ · Ecce concipies in vtero et
paries filiũ: et vocabis nomẽ
eius iħm·Hic erit magn⁹: et fi=
lius altiſſimi vocabit·Et dabit
illi dñs deus ſedem dauid pʃ
eius:et regnabit ī domo iacob
in eternũ: ⁊ regni eius non erit
finis· Dixit aũt maria ad ãge=
lũ·Quõ fiet iſtud· qm virũ nõ
cognoſco:Et reſpõdens ange
lus dixit ei·Spiritus ſanct⁹ ſu

Plate VI The Annunciation (Luke i, 28–35) from the 36-line *Bible*.
British Museum C.9.d.6. *Natural size.*

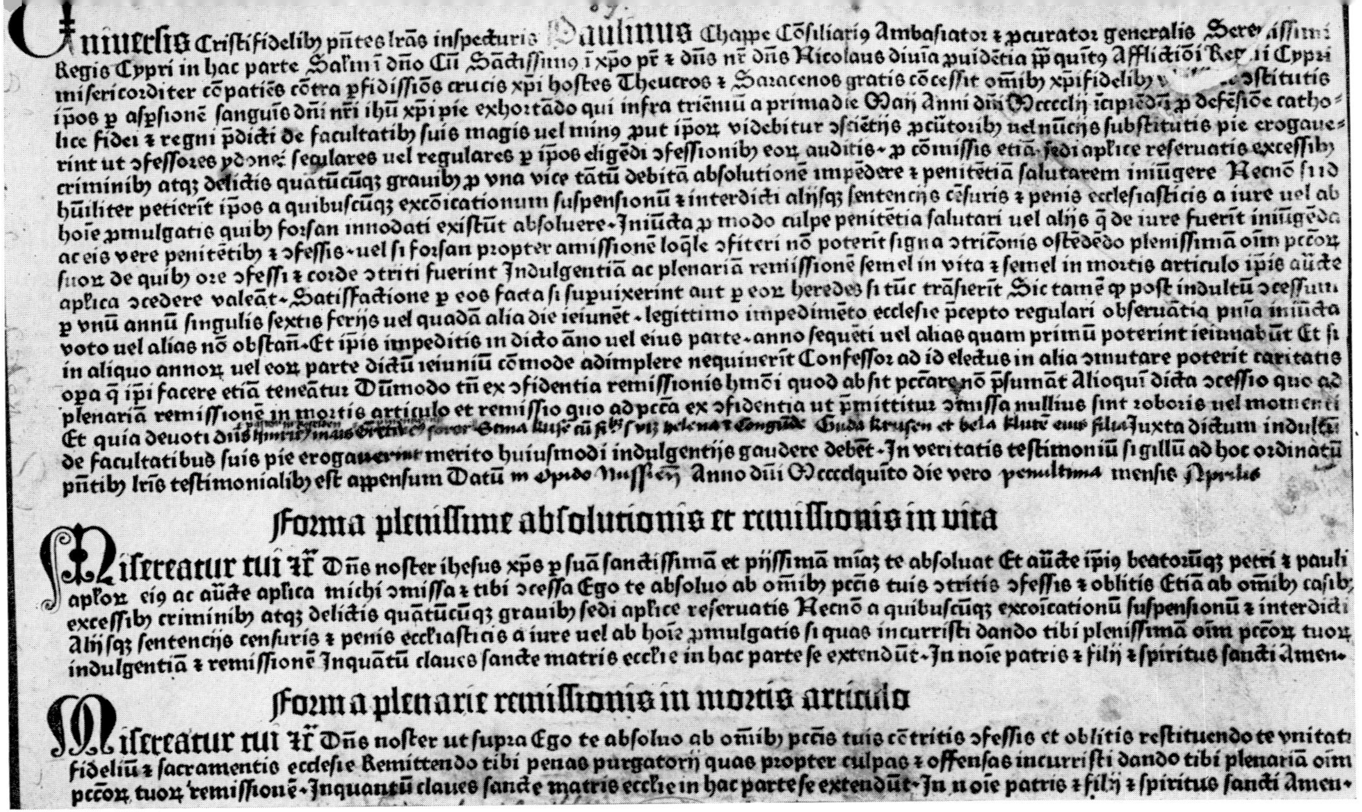

Forma plenissime absolutionis et remissionis in uita

Forma plenarie remissionis in mortis articulo

Plate VII The 30-line *Indulgence* of 1454, in one of the five variant issues which bear the date 1455. The larger type is that of the 42-line *Bible*. This copy was issued, as stated by the manuscript insertions, at Neuss on 29 April 1455 to Henricus Mais and members of his family. British Museum IA.53. *Type-page reduced from 6 x 9½ in.*

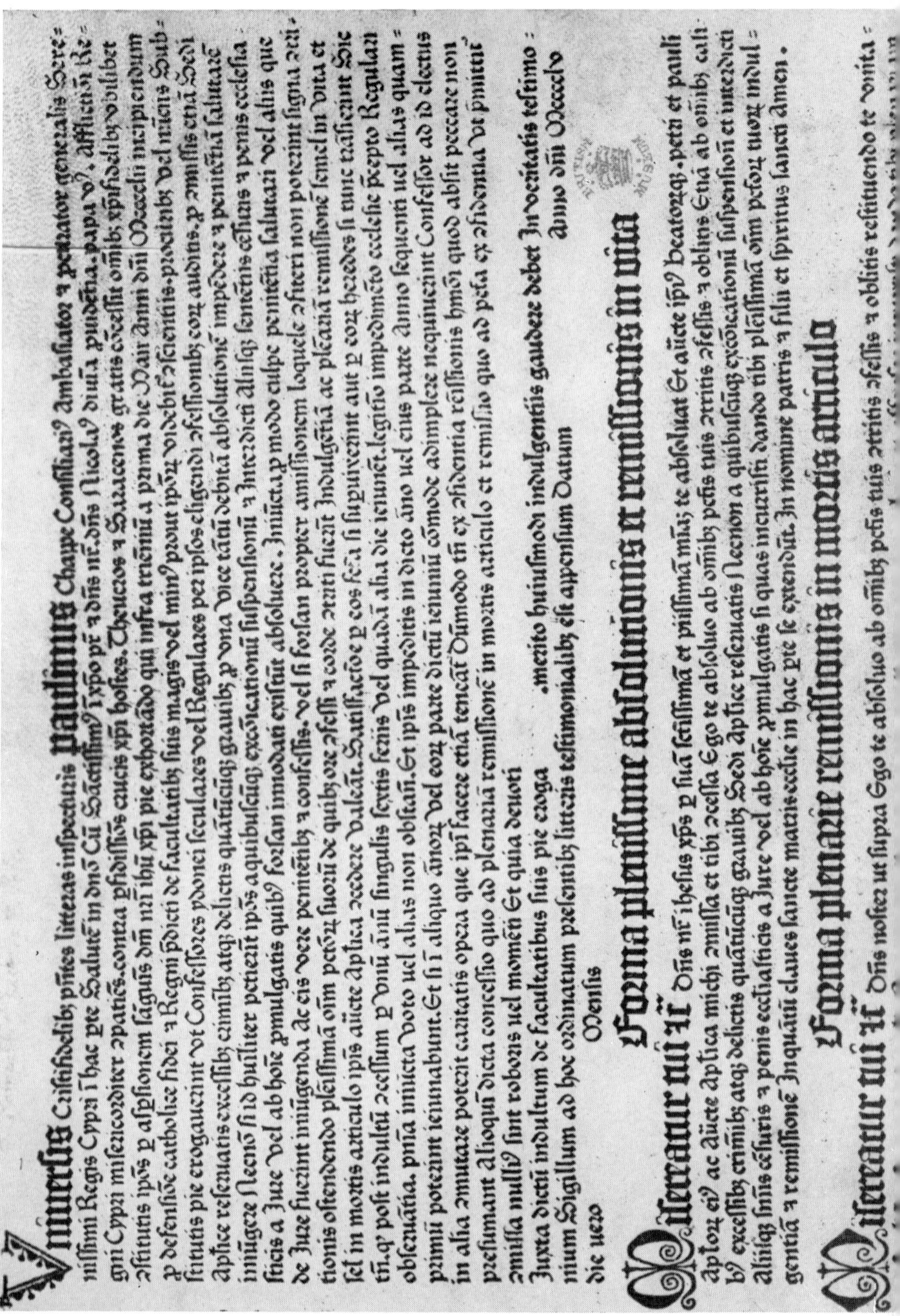

Plate VIII The 31-line *Indulgence* of 1454, in one of the variant issues bearing the date 1455. The large type is that of the 36-line *Bible*. British Museum IA.62. *Type-page reduced from 7 x 9½ in.*

Dñicis diebz post festū trinitatis · Inuitatozium,

siegē magnū dūm venite adozemus, p̄s Uenite ·
Dñicis diebz post festū epḥie Inuitatoziū ·

Adozem⁹ dūm qui fecit nos, p̄ venite aī Seruite ·

Eatus vir qui
non abijt in   Euouae ·
consilio impiozū et in
via pccōz nō stetit: τ in
cathedra pestilēcie nō se=
dit, Sed ī lege dūi vo
lūtas ei⁹: et in lege eius meditabit̄ die ac
nocte, Et erit tanq̄ lignū qd̄ plātatū iste
secus decurlus aq̄z: qd̄ fructū suū dabit in
tpe suo Et foliū ei⁹ nō defluet: τ oīa q̄cūq̄
faciet ṗsṗerabūt, Nō sic impij nō sic sed
tanq̄ puluis quē ṗicit ventus a facie terre,
Ideo non resurgi t impij in iudicio: neqz
pccōzes in cōsilio iustoz Qm noiut dūs
viā iustoz: τ iter impiiz peribit, Gla p̄

Plate IX The first page of the 1457 *Psalter*. Fust and Schoeffer, Mainz, 14 August 1457.
British Museum G.12216. *Type-page reduced from 13 x 8½ in.*

Omenſas omnipotenti deo. pa
tri et filio et ſpūſanctō gͤaͥaͧ referimͧ accͦ
ones. qui nͬū catholicon ex multis et diuſis doc
toͣ texturis elaboratū atͧ contextū licet p̄ mul
ta annoͣ curricula Jn O ͨ lxxxvj anno dñj no
nis marcj ad finem uſͧ pͦuxit Pro quo hoc ſo
luͭ ṁ admodu͠ neceſſarium. a uobis humiliter
depoſco Fratres et dñj mei Jnquͣtū peccͦres fra
tres mei Jnͣntū iuſti dñj mei. quatenus pro me
peccͦte philocalo ad deum p̄ces porrigere uelitis
ut uoſtraͣ precū interuentu. omniuͣ meoͣ a deo
perptͣ uenia peccͦͣ. ad terram apͧcam ad terram
eliſiam .i. extͤ leſionem poſitam. ad padiſi uͣͧelͣͣ
guaudia una uobiſcum ualeam peruenire. ubi reg
nat examuſſim. dñs noſter ihͤſus xp̄s. dei filius
benedcūs Jn cuius nomine flectetur omne genͧ
celeſtium. terreſtrium. et infernoͣ. Cui eſt honor
et gloria magnitudo et magnificenͨia ūtͧs et po
teſtas regnū et imperiuͣ in ſecula ſeculoͣ Amen

Altiſſimi preſidio cuius nutu infantium lingue fi
unt diſerte. Qui ͧ ṅ ioſepe puulis reuelat quod
ſapientibus celat. Dic liber egregius. catholicon.
dñice incarnacionis annis O ccc lx Alma in ur
be maguntina nacionis inclite germanice. Quam
dei demencia tam alto ingenij lumine. dono ͧ ͨ
tuito. ceteris terraͣ nacionibus preferre. illuſtrare
ͧ dignatus eſt ſlon calami. ſtilͥ. aut penne ſuffra
gio. ſ mira patronaͣ formaͣ ͧ conͦodia ͬͣpor
done et modulo. impreſſus atͧ confectus eſt.
Dinc tibi ſancte pater nato cū flamine ſacro. laus
et honor dño trino tribuatur et uno Eccleſie lau
de libro hoc catholice plaude Qui laudare piam
ſemper non linque mariam DEO. GRACIAS

Plate X The *Catholicon*, showing the colophon stating that the book
was printed at Mainz in 1460, 'under the guidance of the Most High,
who often reveals to the simple what he conceals from the wise', and
'without help of pen, stilus or quill but by the marvellous conformity
of punches and types'. British Museum IC.302. *Natural size.*

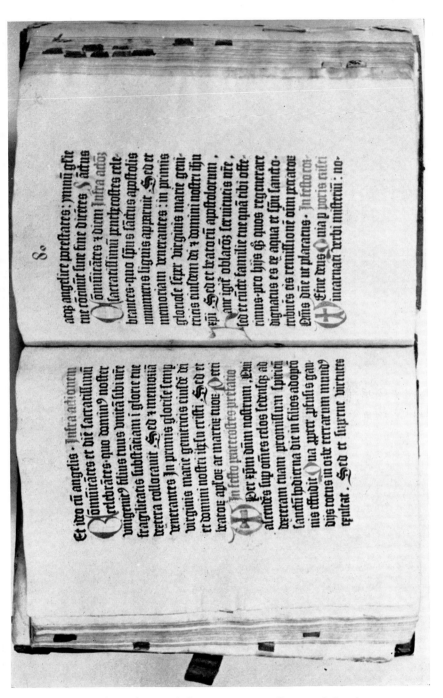

Plate XI The *Missale speciale*, printed about 1473 in an earlier state, designed about 1454, of the smaller of the two types used in the 1457 Mainz *Psalter*. From the Pierpont Morgan Library copy, reproduced by kind permission. *Reduced from a type-page height of c. 8½ in.*

Plate XII Part of leaf v from the first edition of the block-book *Biblia pauperum*, printed *c.* 1465, probably in the Netherlands. Both text and illustrations were produced by rubbing the uppermost side of the paper over an incised wooden block moistened with a water-based ink. British Museum IB.45. *Slightly reduced.*

Noes arche

den gods eñ we gheoezdelß voß tß ewighß kerker Ster bi Syce bermhdcheiß Syn wi bermh-
telic weder gheuriet. Voee waee wi mostē alle gaē intē kerker der hellē der wi mits nie-
mēts hulpe wtgenomē en mochte werdß Da
er tepudē so heeft aengeliē goedertierlic oñse
stact der verdoemnisse die vader der ontferm-
hdcheiß eñ der alınger vtwestinghe eñ geno-
mē ons te vlossē bi hem seluē. op welkß hem
belieft heeft ons te genē een tepkß bi eence
oliuē die vader duuē inder archen den beslote-
nē ghebracht wert Daß betepkßde was die to-
comēde ontfermhertcheit die beslotenen indē
voozgebrocht der hellē Die niet alleen gesey-
nß en wert dß genē die der archē warß. Ster
alle der werlß wert die oliue tenē tepkß der
salicheiß ghegeuē. Eñ daß heeft god voir be-
wesß i veel figurē alse den neerstige stuißt wel
openbaer werß inder heiliger scriften. O goe-
de ihesu leer ons daß wi die heilighe scrijft le-
ren moeten moeten. ende daß wi uwe minne
voß ons verstaē moeten. Amē

Genesis

Plate XIII Leaf 8 recto, second column, of the first Dutch edition of *Speculum
humanae salvationis*, printed *c.* 1471 by an anonymous press perhaps at
Utrecht. The text was printed from movable type in a press; the illustrations,
however, were added separately by means of blocks previously used in a
block-book, and were printed not in a press but by the block-book process
of laying the paper on an incised block and rubbing the uppermost side.
British Museum IB.47000. *Natural size.*

Plate XIV The earliest illustration of a printing-press, from the *Danse Macabre* printed by Mathias Huss, Lyons, 18 February 1499. Note the compositor with case of type, composing-stick and two-page forme, the press-man, his colleague inking a forme with ink-balls, and

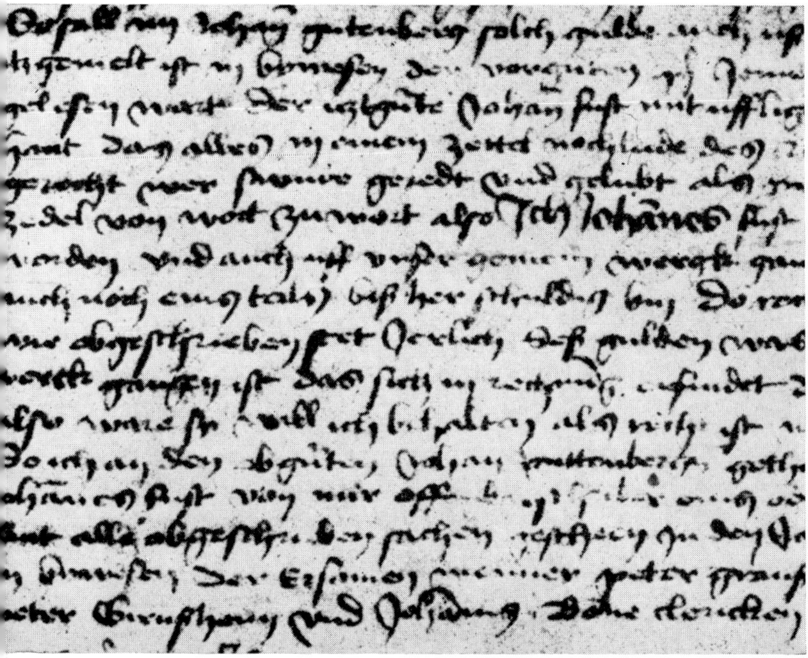

Plate XV A section of the Helmasperger Instrument, a summary, drawn up by the Mainz notary Ulrich Helmasperger, of the Fust *versus* Gutenberg lawsuit on 6 November 1455. Note the names of Gutenberg (lines 1, 12), Fust (lines 3, 6, 13) and Schoeffer ('Peter Girnssheim', line 16). Reproduced by kind permission from a complete facsimile in A. Ruppel, *Johann Gutenberg* (1947), p. 104. *Enlarged.*

Plate XVI A hand-mould for casting type, in the Gutenberg-Museum at Mainz. Reproduced by kind permission from A. Ruppel, *Die Technik Gutenbergs und ihre Vorstufen* (1961).

Plate XVII A hypothetical reconstruction of Gutenberg's press in the Gutenberg-Museum at Mainz showing a pull of the press. Reproduced by kind permission of Prof. Dr. A. Ruppel.

Plate XVIII The same press, showing a two-column page after printing. Reproduced by kind permission from A. Ruppel, *Die Technik Gutenbergs und ihre Vorstufen* (1961).